Never too late to make a U-Turn:
An Educational Pledge & 15 Questions To Self-Development

Copyright © 2005 by Alberto O. Cappas
Published in cooperation with Nubian Voices
NubianSpeakers@aol.com

A Nubian Voices Book

An Excellent Tool for Self-Development:

Parents, Educators, Counselors, and Youth-Serving Professionals

For youth at risk and young people who need to
get out of the Box...

For the people that lifted the top off the "Box"

Allen Clifton Hooks, Educator / Intellectual
For introducing me to Malcolm X, Martin Luther King, Jr., and to Shakespeare

Domingo Rodriguez, Community Activist
For introducing me to community involvement

Hon. Arthur O. Eve, Elected Official
For introducing me to the Democratic political process

Maria Rosa, Educator
For introducing me to the importance of personal hygiene and exercising

John Moffitt, School Teacher/Educator
For introducing me to the Republican Party and the different philosophy between the two major parties

Donald Turchiarelli, Political Consultant
For educating me that there are positive and negative elements in both major political parties

----

And to: John Collins, Jamil Hassan, Donald Anglin, Roosevelt Rhodes, Jose C. Pizarro, Marcelina Rodriguez, Juventino Mejia, Roqui Aguilar, and Michael A. Rivera....
For creating the base that created the journey…
For creative thinking….and love of caring….

Never Too Late To Make a U-Turn:

An Educational Pledge And 15 Questions to Self-Development

Copyright 2005 by Alberto O. Cappas
Printed in the United States of America

ISBN 13: 978-1-4414-1404-5
ISBN 10: 1-4414-1404-5

Acknowledgement

Never Too Late To Make a U-Turn

"An Educational Pledge & 15 Questions to Self-Development"
© **2005**
By Alberto O. Cappas

Alberto O. Cappas is a published writer, author of **"Doña Julia & Other Selected Poems"**, 2003; **"Disintegration of the Puerto Ricans"**, 1997; **Echolalia, Verse & Vibration**, 1987; and **"The Pledge: A Guide for Everyday Living"**, published in 2001. *"Never too late to make a U-turn: An Educational Pledge & 15 Questions Leading to Self-Development"* is designed for students enrolled in the inner-city public school system. It has been widely published in the United States and widely utilized by the educational community, including community based organizations, such as ASPIRA, Urban League, NYC Board of Education, National Association of Puerto Rican Women, Community Action Organization of Buffalo & Erie County, and others.

Alberto's poetry, including **An Educational Pledge**, has been included in numerous anthologies and publications throughout the United States, Canada, and India. Some of the publications include: Guide Press, The Rican Journal, Buffalo Sunday News, El Boricua National Magazine, Black Image Journal, Revista Chicana-Riqueña Anthology, Syracuse Impartial Citizen News, WNET-TV Arts Series, Bearers of Blackness Anthology, Full Circle Anthology, Saludos Hispano Magazine, Viva Magazine, among others.

Table of Content

- About the Book
- Understanding the Need for Balance in our Journey
- 15 Questions to Self-Development
- An Educational Pledge: Commitment to Change
- About the Author
- An Educational Pledge Storefront

About this Book

NEVER TOO LATE TO MAKE A U-TURN
"AN EDUCATIONAL PLEDGE & 15 QUESTIONS TO SELF-DEVELOPMENT"
BY ALBERTO O. CAPPAS

*The book is b*ased on my many years of speaking to young people and others about the need to take control of our lives and not allow politicians, rap musicians (i.e., degrading of women and other negative messages) and drug dealers to make decisions for our paths in life since they are very prominent images and realities that we face everyday in our communities, as well as in the media outlet and fashion industry.

The work is based on educating young people to understand the meaning and definition of **values** and **standards** in one's life. The more we understand its meaning, the more control we will have over the choices we make in life. When one instills these values and standards as a system within oneself, one has a better chance at leading **a more productive and enjoyable journey in his or her lifetime**.

For example, society instills in our young people that they must go to school in order to prepare for a job that would lead to a career. I strongly believe and know from personal experience that we must go much further in convincing our young people why education is so important. Education is very important. However, to share that importance does not have only one "reason". Young people must be made aware of the other dynamics for pursuing an education.

We must instill in our young people that they must go to school for other important reasons such as, learning to read, learning to write, an opportunity to meet other human beings outside their immediate social circle, exposure to the arts, providing the student a stage to be in contact with the world, and an opportunity to be exposed to other cultures and customs.

We need to pay attention to a student's positive hobbies (if they have any or cultivate one based on his/her interest) and see how we can help them make an intellectual and economic connection between the hobbies and the amazing economic and business potential of the hobby. This can prepare our young people to become producers and providers rather than consumers. If we provided this motivation, the dropout rate would be much lower.

I dropped out of high school several times until someone took the time and introduced me to the world of theatre and poetry, giving me a reason to go back to school and pursue my education. I no longer felt as if I was being forced to go to school only to prepare for a job. I became aware that school was a beginning to my personal growth and development, and not to a job. I started to understand the true meaning of the word "education."

"Never Too Late to Make a U-Turn: An Educational Pledge & 15 Questions to Self-Development" provides young readers (i.e., with the help of their teachers, counselors and parents), with the chance and opportunity to visualize these inner qualities at an early stage, to understand that although they do not see it, a conceptual system (system of ideas and concepts) does exist for them to visualize, even within the midst of a negative environment (community). This also works for older students. It is never too late to make a u-turn.

It is important that role models (i.e., teachers, counselors, parents, and youth-serving professionals) help students understand this book and help them to examine their purpose on the planet and begin to discuss and define the meaning of values and standards – essential to one's personal growth and development. There should be no judgments attached. This should be an open conversation where the student knows that there are no "wrong" or "right" answers. It is a time to openly bring out the students' honest comments without judgment from the onset. The facilitator should open the discussion with "non-judgment" as the ground rule.

I first wrote the poem, **The Pledge,** which I used in my poetry readings to young audiences in public schools, colleges, and community organizations. It is designed to serve as a guide to help one understand and navigate the daily encounters and activities in our lives. **The Pledge**, as a stand-alone poem, has been widely published in newspapers, magazines, flyers, book form, bookmark, Internet, and widely used by individuals and organizations.

The direct audience for this book is the young people in urban communities, students and their parents, school counselors, teachers, and educational consultants.

Individual students can utilize this book as an everyday guide. It can be used as a one-on-one counseling tool by the teacher, counselor or parent, and it can also be used in groups and in workshop settings.

Understanding the need for **Balance** in our Journey

The real secret to a successful Life!

Understanding the need for Balance in our Journey

I hope to have an opportunity to help you light up the areas you need to light up, as well as to turn off the areas you need to turn off. It is my belief that to succeed in life, to enjoy the time we spend on this planet, to be in control of where we need to be or where we plan to be or where we would like to be, we first need to have a plan of balance in our lives.

Balance is a part of the purpose for our journey. I have been able to lead a decent and honorable life, doing several things that in the scheme of this life do not seem to go together, especially when it comes to functioning as a poet/writer, community activist, as well as an entrepreneur and municipal government employee.

Early in my career, when I lived in Buffalo, NY, I served as a Deputy Commissioner for the NYS Division for Youth. Today, I'm still connected with local government where I work as Director of Community Affairs for the New York City Human Resources Administration (HRA). This is an important yet massive agency, which is responsible for providing services to one of the largest cities in the world. How did I get to this position of responsibility and public service? The key is Balance. I was born in Puerto Rico, raised in NYC, in a single parent household. My home life consisted of five sisters and two brothers, all raised under the influence and negative images of welfare, food stamps, government cheese, and peanut butter.

At an early age I found myself on the receiving end as a consumer of government's public assistance programs.

My outside environment included gangs on every corner recruiting new victims. I experienced people drinking themselves to death, lovers betraying each other, and young people destroying their lives with drugs. I witnessed Puerto Ricans and Blacks coming together to form gangs to fight other Puerto Ricans and Blacks.

I witnessed many of my peers dropping out of school, denouncing education and refusing to learn and advance themselves.

Education was not cool – so my neighborhood friends elected to stay in the Box. By the "Box", I mean the manipulation of their lives without their input which started very early, and one of many negative decisions and choices made in their early life period. The Box is an extension of ignorance and personal apathy. It is an invisible but powerful force, a system of mental traffic signs directing and pushing you in different directions without your full awareness or approval. …

A State of Mind…

Once within the "Box", the captive are without a concrete philosophical or spiritual purpose. This is a dangerous imbalance.

I was fortunate that at an early age I was able to see things clearly. It took me awhile to understand and properly use this clear vision. I knew that something was not right, something was terribly wrong in the way we were just living our lives from day-to-day, without thinking of the impact of our decisions and choices. I was inside the Box.

I knew that the Italians and Irish families all had jobs. My family was on welfare. My Black and

Hispanic friends were also on welfare. We accepted the government Cheese, the Ham, the dry Milk and the Peanut Butter, as well as the Black pair of shoes we used to get once a year. We never questioned why? We were a complete mess and we did not know it!

We were inside the Box!

Even today, many of us are still inside the Box, and still on the road to nowhere! This is a dangerous imbalance! As a Puerto Rican coming to a new land, a new language, and a cold climate, I became uncertain of my presence in the USA Mainland, uncertain of my worth as a human being and in the process of dealing with USA Mainland institutions, I lost my identity of who I was as a Puerto Rican and consequently, also lost my self-esteem and eventually started disliking myself. This is a dangerous imbalance.

Fortunately, the self-hatred did not last long...

Due to not going to school, I was labeled a PIN (Person in Need of Supervision) at the age of fourteen. The Juvenile Justice System confined me to reform school for about ten months, somewhere in upstate NY (a place called Warwick State Training School for Boys) where everything was green, removing me from the destructive street elements. For me, it was not just a geographic change. The experience of going/moving from New York City streets to a new environmental setting in upstate NY opened a door to a whole new world. At that moment, I realized that the world was composed of many parts, and not just the streets that were consuming me.

When I was in public school, I used to read about "Dick and Jane", thinking they were a figment of someone's imagination because their lives and neighborhood was nothing like mine. But I found out that they were real, along with the beautiful Barns, Cows, Pigs and Horses. This was the beginning of developing my inner structure for Balance!

I also learned that I was a pretty smart and creative individual. While in confinement, many of the White, Black and Latino youth paid me in cigarettes and other items for me to write love letters to their girlfriends and to their parents.

That was an educational and intellectual awakening for me, to have all these people come to me to write or read for them due to their inability to read or write. This experience alone broke the "colonial mentality" inside of me. The lack of self-esteem and self-hatred literally disappeared completely. This was for me a regaining of Balance!

As great as this country is, many of us have lost sight of the true values of one's life journey, placing too much emphasis on financial needs over one's need for good health, good friends, social enjoyment, spending quality time with our family members, and truly enjoying the work or career we find ourselves. Balance!

We should truly listen to the saying: "You can't pay me enough to be miserable." Hear it? Think about it! If we don't know the meaning of that, let us become wise and begin to learn the essence of the words before our journey comes to an end. It is never too late to make a "U-turn" to regain our Balance!

I know too many people who now regret holding on to their twenty year plus jobs in order to be eligible for retirement and a pension plan. In waiting for the pension plan, they grew old and tired, letting dreams pass them by, allowing them to disappear. If they had to do it again, they would take the risk, and not the stability of a 9 to 5. Balance!

We also make decisions for the wrong reasons, and we pick choices for the wrong reasons. For example, I want more money so I will take a job that would pay me more, knowing full well that I will be miserable in the job, leading to stress and perhaps leading to some form of depression and other emotional and health disaster. This is a dangerous imbalance.

We need clarity of vision of who we are in relation to our presence on this planet. We need to identify and understand our purpose. It is not enough to live from day-to-day without examining one's life's journey of choices and decisions. To not examine oneself is a dangerous imbalance.

For example, many people who go into business work on developing a business plan, a blueprint to help them navigate the healthy growth of the business. Just as important for our life's journey, we need to also develop a plan for ourselves. We need to know where we want to go and how to get there. Take a few moments and reflect on the fifteen questions I prepared for you in the next section of this book.

If you have not asked yourself the 15 questions I prepared for you, I recommend that you begin now, and take personal notes with which to reflect upon. It is never too late to begin living your life as it was supposed to be lived. If you are interested in making money, look at your hobbies and see if you can begin to turn them into a positive, rewarding business venture. We need to work to live, not live to work, which is what many of us do. This is a dangerous imbalance.

We need to understand ourselves before trying to understand others.

Use the fifteen questions to improve the potential of your vision that will help you transform your life and establish an inner structure that depends on a system of **personal**

value-centered awareness. Once you get out the Box and become liberated, you can begin to live your purpose; and part of that purpose is for you to reach out and help other people get out the Box! The magic to life is to give, not take! But you must first be free to have that power.

You will be able to sing with the wind without being blown away, dance with the Sun without getting burned, and to have a positive impact on the lives of those you come into contact with. Balance always gives you pure and positive energy. Before I jumped out the Box, I used to focus on material things, making money and looking good on the outside while my balance of health and happiness was taking a beating. This was a dangerous imbalance.

I have utilized my life experiences to help establish an inner structure that depends on a system of **personal value-centered awareness**.

I have come to understand that when it rains, there is a purpose why it rains. Learn to turn your scars into stars.

When I experience joy I know that it was my encounter with sadness that provided me an opportunity to better appreciate joy.

I know that when I laugh there also will be occasions when I will have to cry.

And I know that when faced with the decision between a positive opportunity and a positive risk, I will take the risk. But know that "risk" is not impulse. It is the choice we make based on the truth we want to live.

I turned to my life experiences, looking at my strength and weaknesses to help navigate my journey.

Balance is living your true purpose on the planet! I did my studies at the State University of New York at Buffalo (SUNYAB). As a student, I learned more outside the classroom then I did inside. I was a student leader, and I was the founder of the Puerto Rican Student organization, *Puerto Rican Organization for Dignity, Elevation, and Responsibility* (PODER). As a student leader, I joined forces with African Americans and other students. We were able to convince the university to establish an Office of Minority Student Affairs (OMSA). The office served as a link to connect the university's contacts and resources to the minority students and to the local minority community needs. The office was established and I graduated with my BA degree that same year, and was offered the position of Assistant to the Vice President for Student Affairs, appointed as the Associate Director of OMSA. I accepted and I used that position to educate myself, to learn about management, administration, and resources. I was then able to establish a relationship with the community's leading African American and Latino leaders and elected officials.

In addition, because I was the liaison to the African American and Latino student organizations, I had an opportunity to work with them on the development of workshops and conferences. My responsibility was to assist them in finding appropriate African American and Latino speakers/lecturers to bring to the campus. My job was to locate or contact the existing Speakers' Bureau that represented these speakers. I found that most bureaus had few African American or Latino speakers.

Because of this, I found myself directly contacting African American and Hispanic poets, writers, elected officials, and business leaders.

After twelve years at SUNYAB, I retired and completely divorced myself from higher education but always kept the idea of a speaker's bureau in the back of my mind. Twenty plus years later, I used that college experience to create the first Black & Latino Speakers Bureau in the country, "AOC Speakers and Consultants", which I established in 1991. Today, in addition to AOC, I am also the co-founder of "Nubian Speakers", a speaker's bureau that represents African American Speakers.

I am also the founder of Don Pedro Cookies (DPC), still in development as a positive Hispanic role model company providing scholarships and business ventures for youth. It will be marketed in New York City, with plans to approach other markets once we establish a base of loyalty and contracts in New York State.

The DPC venture is not solely based on my motives to make money. It is based on my commitment to education and my commitment to make a difference in the lives of children. Balance!

What is Don Pedro Cookies and where did this business idea come from? DPC is a reflection of my life's experience. When I was growing up, there were no Don Pedro Cookies or Hispanic products for me to relate to showing positive Puerto Rican or Hispanic role models. There were no positive characters available to re-enforce or support my journey. There was no one telling me that education was an important key that would open the door to the world. DPC provides something for all those concerns. The Cookies are based on a positive character, "Don Pedro", one that supports and re-enforces the importance of education. DPC is a new/start-up operation.

My plan is simply to continue to enjoy living my life. I have always focused on the idea "to serve", and when that idea is executed with "care and love", harmony comes your way.

If your goal is to only make money, then you may meet that goal, but ask yourself: "Will you have joy and harmony in your life." You will miss the Balance!

If you can find it in you to learn to stay focused, and work to prepare a plan for your life journey, and you sincerely make sure to include your purpose to serve, destiny will come to support your efforts.

You will have the harmony, good health and the music that only you can hear because it was written and composed only by you – for your journey! If you hear the music, you found your purpose! I dare and challenge you to work on your Balance. God meant for you to enjoy the wonders of life with a base of spiritual balance.

Go and enjoy the music!

The Questions
Strategies to get out of the "Box"

Introduction: 15 Questions To Self-Development

The following fifteen questions are designed to help with your self-development process. The questions also will work to develop clarity of vision of who you are in relation to your presence on this planet.

It is not enough to live from day-to-day without examining one's life's journey of choices and decisions.

Take the time and provide answers to the following questions. If addressed seriously, these fifteen questions will help to enhance your purpose and quality of Life.

Learn to truly appreciate why you are a living creature on this planet!

Get out of the "Box" – and be you!

1
Who am I?

Use this question to challenge yourself to truly examine what you have become since your day of birth. Begin to see how you can carve out the real you…

Notes

2
Why am I here?

Give thoughts to the reason why you were born. Is it an accident, or is there a spiritual or divine purpose for your existence? Are you here to give or to take? Take a good look at the events of the world and how you are linked and connected to them.

Notes

3

Am I living out my dreams?
Do I have dreams?
If not, why?

Are you working as a doorman but want to be a painter? Are you living in Buffalo but want to be in New York City? Are you employed in a job that you dislike but stay just to collect retirement benefits after twenty years on the job? Do not let your dreams pass you by. Get on your skates and move on! Take the risk!

Notes

4

Am I doing what I want to be doing with my life?

Instead of saying: "I hope my dreams come true", why not say: "I will work and plan to make my dreams come true." There is a reason for dreaming. Dreams are like blueprints and designs. Do not let your dreams remain dreams. Bring them to life.

Notes

5

Am I living a life based on other people's expectations?

Do what you need to be doing, and not what others want you to do. Remember that the expectations must come from you, and not from anyone else. You are the gatekeeper of your aspirations on this planet. The expectations are yours to design and navigate.

Notes

6

Am I happy? If yes, why am I happy? If not, why?

Make up your mind to be happy. Do not allow or give power away to others to direct and control your emotions. Control your ego, understand the influence of family, and appreciate your association with the Universe. Smile with the Sun, not at the Sun. Dance with the Moon, not at the Moon. Be happy!

Notes

7

Is my present situation based on a risk taken or on an opportunity provided?

Are you cruising in life, taking anything that comes your way without an honest examination of yourself in relation to these opportunities? Take the time to think about things you would truly like to be doing and what you need to do to get there. You need to enjoy the element of Risk and let go of what you now have so you can move forward with your real purpose and mission.

Notes

8

Where do I expect to be in the next 10 to 15 years?

Stop cruising and begin to see yourself 5, 10, and 15 years from now. What do you see? What would you like to see? At this very moment is the right time to plan seeds for your Tree so you can enjoy the Fruits of your labor tomorrow. Begin investing today. Tomorrow never comes for those that don't take the time to design it.

Notes

9

Have I maintained a system of values and standards to govern my life?

How do you live your life from day to day? Is there something inside of you that stops you from doing something you don't want to do? How do you arrive at making important decisions or choices? Have you taken the time to examine your inner constitution and amendments?

Notes

10

Am I a consumer or a provider? Do I know the difference between the two?

A consumer consumes (takes). A provider provides (gives). You need to address this question very seriously if you want to move to a higher level of awareness and consciousness. The answer you find will be a big step in formulating the way you decide to live your life.

Notes

11

What are my strengths and weaknesses as a human being?

You need to seriously look at yourself and determine the strengths and weaknesses of your human tools. For example, if you hate or dislike reading, you would not want to take a job as an editor or proofreader even if the pay is great. Use your strengths to get where you need to go, as well as to understand your weaknesses. As human beings we all have them. The more we learn about ourselves, the sooner we get where we want to go. Read, use the computer, attend lectures, and ask questions. Just get started.

12

What are my hobbies? Do I have any positive hobbies? If not, why?

Take the time to understand the origin of your interest in hobbies. Hobbies can be an extension of your purpose and mission on this planet. Properly utilized, hobbies can help you with your personal growth and development as a person.

Notes

13

Have I explored the potential of my hobbies?

Hobbies are sometimes hidden treasures that can lead to a career or business enterprise. Get to understand the value of your hobbies and examine how they can help you grow and develop spiritually and economically.

Notes

14

Do I understand the difference between being religious and being spiritual?

Many people believe in God. They attend church for their religious guidance. Others do not attend a church but also believe, taking upon themselves the need to reach out and talk directly to God or the Supreme Being. What about you? Are you a religious person? Are you a spiritual person? Can you be both?

Notes

15

When I look in the mirror, what do I see? Am I able to honestly verbalize that image? If not, why?

Be happy with who you are. Understand your mind and your body; look into the spirit and the soul of your being. Use this question to confront the real you and work to obtain the highest level of self-awareness about the person you are capable of becoming. Have the courage to say goodbye to your negative associations as well as to negative habits. As long as you are alive, you are still in the game of life. Play by the rules, and use your inner constitution and amendments to guide you in the journey…

BEGIN THE PROCESS TO GET OUT THE BOX!

The one you were placed in without your permission…

If you have not asked yourself similar questions to these, I recommend that you begin now. As you do, take personal notes with which to reflect upon. It is never too late to begin living your life as it was supposed to be lived. Everyday is a gift to start again…

We need to understand ourselves before trying to understand others. Review these questions and use them to understand and improve the potential of your "vision", a vision that will help you transform your life and help you to establish an inner structure that depends on a system of personal value-centered awareness. **It is never too late to make a u-turn… Time to make The Pledge…**

An Educational Pledge

The Commitment To Make The Change

An Educational Pledge

I PLEDGE TO MAINTAIN A
HEALTHY MIND AND BODY
STAYING AWAY FROM THE VICE OF DRUGS
I PLEDGE ALWAYS TO TRY MY BEST TO
UNDERSTAND
THE IMPORTANCE OF KNOWLEDGE AND
EDUCATION
I PLEDGE TO PAINT A POSITIVE PICTURE OF
WHERE I PLAN TO BE IN THE FUTURE
NOT ALLOWING OBSTACLES TO STOP THE
GROWTH OF MY PLANS
I PLEDGE TO SEEK ANSWERS TO QUESTIONS,
WITH THE UNDERSTANDING THAT THEY
WILL LEAD TO OTHER DISCOVERIES
I PLEDGE TO WORK FIRM
WITH THE AWARENESS AND CONFIDENCE
THAT FIRM WORK TODAY WILL SERVE

As the Seeds for my strong Tree
tomorrow
A Tree that no one will be able to tear
down
I pledge to learn proper languages,
Beginning with my Mother's
Always prepared to Appreciate others
I pledge to gain a better understanding
of Me
By understanding my
Cultural Roots
I pledge to fully accept Me as a
Human being
A Rainbow of
Many cultures and colors
I pledge to overcome any Personal
misfortunes
Becoming Stronger from such
misfortunes
Always striving to become
A wise person...

Get out of the "Box"

Other Books by Alberto O. Cappas

- Lessons for Myself, 2009
- Doña Julia & Other Selected Poems, 2002
- The Pledge: A Guide for Everyday Living, 2000
- Disintegration of the Puerto Ricans, 1997
- Echolalia, Verse & Vibration, 1987
- Echoes, 1983

An Educational Pledge Storefront

An *Educational Pledge* has become a positive message for young people. It has been included in numerous publications as well as utilized by many groups and organizations throughout the USA. An Educational Pledge is now available in selected marketing and promotional items for schools and institutions. Contact us for information on how to place your order:

Items:

- Coffee Mug
- Mouse Pad
- T-shirt
- Bookmark
- Tote Bag
- Certificate
- Poster (laminated)
- Magnet

Ask about our Spanish version:
Una Promesa Educacional
for non-English speaking community.
The Spanish version was translated by Coral Caporale,
an Educational and Cultural Consultant.

ThePledgePromesa@aol.com
Tel. 212-860-2019

"Work on your PLAN"

About The Author

Poetry / Inspiration / Education / Philosophy
Classroom Interaction / Workshop

Alberto O. Cappas is a published writer, author of **"Doña Julia & Other Selected Poems"**, 2003; "Disintegration of the Puerto Ricans", 1997; **Echolalia, Verse & Vibration**, 1987; and "**The Pledge: A Guide for everyday living**", published in 2001. The Educational Pledge is designed for students enrolled in the inner-city public school system. Both, the English and Spanish versions, have been widely published in the United States and widely used by the educational community, including community- based organizations.

Alberto's poetry has been included in numerous anthologies and publications throughout the United States, Canada, and India.

Alberto is the Director of Community Affairs for the NYC Human Resources Administration; publisher/founder of The New Tomorrow (TNT), a monthly publication for African American and Latino students; founder of Don Pedro Cookies; and, founder of Nubian Speakers, a speaker's bureau marketing African American & Latino professionals, including poets and writers.

Photo by Eddie Aguilar, co-founder, PuertoRicans.com

**Help us in the war against Ignorance!
One cannot keep hope alive if no plan of action is in place...**

THE AUTHOR'S DREAM

TO FIND A CORPORATE SPONSOR AND PARTNER TO PLACE
AN EDUCATIONAL PLEDGE
-AS A LARGE ADVERTISEMENT-
ON A LARGE BILLBOARD IN TIMES SQUARE
Making it available to the children and youth of the world…helping in the fight against ignorance…

A phone call and email away:

Tel. 212-860-2019
ThePledgePromesa@aol.com

Contact the Author

Alberto O. Cappas

cappas@aol.com

NubianSpeakers@aol.com

www.educationalpledge.com

Made in the USA
Charleston, SC
06 October 2015